Merry Christmas
Joe-Kim
2023
Love thy
Neighbors!

Gettin' Squirrelly

a day in the life of nature's most curious creatures

Gettin' Squirrelly

a day in the life of nature's most curious creatures

WILLOW CREEK PRESS®

Published by Willow Creek Press, Inc.
P.O. Box 147, Minocqua, Wisconsin 54548

All photos © Geert Weggen

Printed in China

The year in the life of a squirrel... What is it like?
Does it live up to the hype? Of course it does. Behind
the bushy tails, world-class nut stashes, and crazy aerial
antics, squirrels are sophisticated social creatures that
enjoy time with friends, boundless curiosity and, in
general, are connoisseurs of the finer things that nature
can provide. Consider this tome a window to the nutty
world of enlightenment, intrigue and occasional
daily drudgery, otherwise known as my life.

spring

Spring is upon us, and boy, does it smell sweet after not seeing green for six months. Every squirrel worth their salt knows that without hard work nothing grows but weeds.

the Earth
LAUGHS
in flowers

In winter, I plot and plan.
In spring, I move.

H. hortensis (garden).* Common Hydrangea. in colour (according to the soil in which the pla posed in ample corymbs or cymes, all differ few. April to September. *l.* broadly-ovate, ser *h.* 2ft. to 5ft. China, 1790. SYN. *Horten* Fig. 252. The varieties of this species are the most noteworthy being "Thomas Hogg"

spring cleaning

* Rake
* Plant this years' food
* Move rocks
* Organize fallen twigs
* Enjoy the sunshine

Nothing like a little laundry on the line to kick off springtime. So fresh and so clean!

We squirrels pride ourselves on being environmentally conscious creatures... why run the dryer when you have warm sunshine and a light breeze? Sayonara winter wardrobe!

'tis the season to be married

Ahh, wedding season! It's so exciting to be a part of a couple's Happily Ever After. The music, the food, getting all gussied up... it's the bees knees. After all my years in the wedding party ranks, maybe I'll decide to try and catch the bouquet this year... Daa dum da dum, daa dum da dum...

The best thing one can do when it's raining is to let it rain. It allows birth, growth, and change. Without rain there is no life, so it's something we squirrels embrace. If it ruins our day and saves our growing season, why should we stop it? So, spring, grace us with your raindrops! With this season, we know the best is yet to come!

april showers
BRING MAY FLOWERS

Don't sneeze!
Ah-ah-ah-chooooo! Well,
it seemed like a good
idea when I first stuck
my nose in it... better
make some wishes!

Spring brings all the beautiful smells and colors that make me smile and spend time outside. Who cares about a little mud with all the life around us... Where flowers bloom so does hope!

Squirrels are known for scampering through the woods and catapulting off of trees, but I prefer flowers in the spring. You can't beat the view or the aroma.

And into the forest I go,
to lose my mind and find my soul.

Of all the paths
you take in life
make sure a few of them
are dirt.

So many people think Easter is about bunnies, chicks and lambs, but you know what... it's about squirrels too! We love hanging with our peeps, taking inventory of our nest eggs and hippity-hopping through the forest.

When strawberries are in season at the
farmers market, picnics are bound to happen.

Hi-ho Nutterbutter, away! You know what they say, to ride on a horse is to fly without wings. We make a good team.

On slower days, we take the canter down to a trot through the woodland trails. You never know what you might see on any given day.

After a long winter of being holed up away from the world, I crave a little adventure. I know it sounds nuts, but cruising through the countryside with the wind in my ears is good for a squirrel's soul!

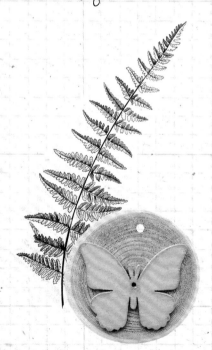

Fore! As soon as the greens start to shape up, it really gets me moving. I've been a little rusty with this game they call golf, but hopefully this season I will make par.

Summer is also the best time to hone my archery skills. My form might leave something to be desired, but I whittled that arrow with my teeth... talk about craftsmanship!

If summer isn't the time to get a little squirrelly, I don't know what is.
Mischievous shenanigans are always more fun when the sun is shining.

Despite what you've probably heard, squirrels actually value family ties just as much as the next fur-bearing mammal. Chats with my Meemaw and Pawpaw are one of the highlights of the summer. Standing around the phone booth gets a little too brisk in the winter when neither of us wants to hang up first.

Meemaw

Pawpaw

summer lovin'

Today was one of those peaceful, serene days, just the lake, my boat, me and the fish. I would cast, catch a fish, and cast and catch a fish. Ahhh, the squirrel days of summer... Remember, good things come to those who bait!

current PLAYLIST

* Everybody Loves A Nut -Johnny Cash
* Trees -21 Pilots
* Born Country -Alabama
* Apple Blossom -The White Stripes
* No Roots -Alice Merton
* Songs from the Wood -Jethro Tull

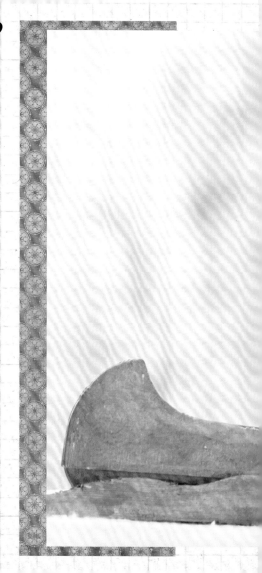

Enjoy the little things in life,
because one day
you will look back,
and realize they were the
big things.

Summer is also the time to get
things off my bucket list. I'm always
up for an adventure or road trip
with friends.

After all that hustle and bustle, I'm in need of some R&R. Thank goodness for my relaxing hammock! Keep calm and hammock on!

Weekends are spent at the beach flexing my muscles for the squirrel girls and working on my color. Hopefully, I am bronzed by the end of the season!

I love to host summer tennis matches. It's my hobby, and boy do I get a workout! One day, I dream of going to Wimbledon. But, for now yard tennis will have to do! You only get to live once, but you get to serve twice!

WIMBLEDON

autumn

I love fall foraging. Autumn
is the time of change in the
woodlands. I stumble on the
best surprises of mushrooms
which I add to my forest
table harvest menu!

Winter is an etching,
spring a watercolor,
summer an oil painting,
and autumn a mosaic
of them all.

Mushrooms aren't the only delight found in the woods; I also gather apples which are juicy and ripe this time of year. You should try my pies!

Look mom, no hands! I'm seriously falling for this weather. Autumn is the time to take risks. With nothing to lose before the winter season, why not take a bite into the most red, plump apple that is calling my name?

favorite BERRIES

- Strawberries
- Blackberries
- Blueberries
- Raspberries
- Mulberries

It's a bird, it's a plane, it's super squirrel.

current MUSIC

Autumn Lullaby
-Natalie Merchant
The squirrel keeps warm
in his furs of gray,
'Neath feathers, birdies
are tucked away,
In yellow jackets, the bees
sleep tight
And cuddle close through
the chilly night,
My baby's snug in her
gown of white.

I have to gather not only food, but wood to keep me warm all winter. This is a grueling process and has to be done in Fall. You have to split the firewood by hand, haul it and stack it. But I will not regret this once the snow flies! Nothing like hunkering down with a warm fire because of the work I did now.

There is NO PLACE LIKE Home

The secret of change
is to focus
all of your energy,
not on fighting the old,
but on building the new.

I have to prepare the homestead too. I never want a chilly surprise, so taking extra precautions allows me to have a cozy winter. I tinker, work and store, getting as prepared as I can before the long months ahead of me!

Dreams don't work
unless you do.

The weight on my scale is nothing compared to the the weight on my shoulders, knowing that winter is going to be here to stay soon. Full bellies and warm paws is the ultimate goal. Steinbeck should have said, "What good is FALL without the cold of winter to give it sweetness?"

Happy Fall Y'all

Don't you worry my little nut babies, I'll use every little nook and cranny to store this year's harvest so nothing goes to waste. Nothing like the taste of hard work paying off!

monday
gather nuts.

tuesday
gather nuts.

wednesday
gather nuts.

thursday
gather nuts.

friday
gather nuts.

saturday
gather nuts.

sunday
gather nuts.

Some days you end up with a hard nut to crack, but all it takes is a little squirrel elbow grease with the right kind of leverage to make life all that it's cracked up to be!

If life gives you nuts then be a nutcracker.

If at first
you don't succeed,
try, try
try again.

favorite NUTS

- Acorns
- Walnuts
- Pecans
- Hickory Nuts
- Almonds
- Hazelnuts
- Peanuts

Sometimes I have to be old school in my methods to complete the task! You know what they say, it's new, it's improved, it's old-fashioned, and it finishes the job!

So, I'm sitting around the other day, just cracking some nuts, when my buddy pops up with this brilliant idea to maximize our winter stash... Who knew he had ideas?

We've been working day and night... it's a good thing his diagram was so detailed. Wish I could say more, but I've taken an oath of silence... can't let this fall into the wrong paws. Can a squirrel apply for a patent?

With all that work, we still add in a little playtime! We love to enjoy the beautiful colors of the forest, and have a little fun during harvest time! Autumn is the time of change!

autumn
leaves and
pumpkins
please

Let it snow

take a dance class

get my fortune read

Now that winter is upon us, so is the extra time. I finally have the freedom to learn, and appreciate all those little things I have been putting off.

Do not be afraid to fail.
Be afraid
not to try.

learn to sew

get a second job

learn to play chess

take an acting class

I don't know what all the fuss is about... who wants to drive themselves crazy all fall and then sleep all winter? Not this squirrel! In addition to my plowing responsibilities, I'm also keeping tabs on these enormous socks... seriously, have you ever seen socks so big? I'm sure I could use them for something... but what?!

Winter is the time to try something new. I worked on my brass, percussion and woodwind instruments! But on a sunny day when the birds start to sing, I will head outside and join in the chorus!

What is wrong with that little yellow bird not wanting to enjoy my band? Hopefully I wasn't harping on him too much?

Do-Re-Mi-fa-so-la-ti-do!

the greatest showman

The lights go dim; you hear the rustle of the crowd, and my heart pounding. I am going to do it! My greatest stunt of all time! 3,2,1... here I go!

ADMIT ONE

019959

Nothing like swinging onto the next thing in life. You know me, if there is an opportunity I will take it!

What's life without a little risk?

No one ever made a difference
by being like everyone else.

Everything you want

is on the other side

of fear.

winter
WONDERLAND

Not only do my friends call me the Picasso, but designing, sculpting and building my winter structures are a way to keep my hands warm. I couldn't do it alone. It takes teamwork and hard work!

May the best of your todays
be the worst of your tomorrows.

cuddle
WEATHER

You would think the shorter days of winter would bore me. But no! I like to stay busy.

feet and he beca
Snow queen might
of

drink
en to

with the red berries the
waiting for them, and he
young reindeer with him, w
ll. The children drank her
sed her About pauto. Then

home and jo
appy man;
lothes for them and prepared her
indeer their side, to the
untry; the first green b
hey said "Good-bye" to the rei
woman. They heard the fir

My friends and I love to make forts, build snowmen, and get a little goofy! I just might be the first one to throw a snowball!

favorite
SONG LYRICS

Be like the squirrel, girl
Be like the squirrel
Give it a whirl, girl
Be like the squirrel

bonfire
& CHILL

But at the end of the day of cold play, we love to warm up by a toasty fire!

I never forget to mail out my holiday cards. The joy and love it spreads into their homes is worth licking every single envelope. Hopefully my letter gets to the North Pole too!

I always say I am going to start my shopping early, but somehow I ALWAYS become that last minute scrambler! You forget all the people you have to buy for and more importantly, where do I put them to hide them from everyone?! Oh the Christmas Chaos!

christmas
WISH LIST

* stainless steel nutcracker
* wire comb
* nut-of-the-month club
* electric hedge trimmer

My tree is one of my prized possessions. The fact that it came from the forest around me and that I could decorate it with all the magic and hope warms even the coldest of winter days! Happy Holidays everyone!